LEGENDARY LIVES

Michael Jordan

by Kate Moening
Illustrated by Claudia Marianno

BELLWETHER MEDIA
MINNEAPOLIS, MN

BLASTOFF! MISSIONS

Blastoff! Missions takes you on a learning adventure! Colorful illustrations and exciting narratives highlight cool facts about our world and beyond. Read the mission goals and follow the narrative to gain knowledge, build reading skills, and have fun!

Traditional Nonfiction

Narrative Nonfiction

Blastoff! Universe

MISSION GOALS

> FIND YOUR SIGHT WORDS IN THE BOOK.

> LEARN ABOUT MICHAEL JORDAN'S LIFE.

> LEARN HOW MICHAEL JORDAN INSPIRES OTHERS TO BE THEIR BEST.

This edition first published in 2026 by Bellwether Media, Inc.

No part of this publication may be reproduced in whole or in part without written permission of the publisher. For information regarding permission, write to Bellwether Media, Inc., Attention: Permissions Department, 3500 American Blvd W, Suite 150, Bloomington, MN 55431.

Library of Congress Cataloging-in-Publication Data

LC record for Michael Jordan available at: https://lccn.loc.gov/2025018585

Text copyright © 2026 by Bellwether Media, Inc. BLASTOFF! MISSIONS and associated logos are trademarks and/or registered trademarks of Bellwether Media, Inc. Bellwether Media is a division of FlutterBee Education Group.

Editor: Rebecca Sabelko   Designer: Andrea Schneider

Printed in the United States of America, North Mankato, MN.

This is **Blastoff Jimmy**! He is here to help you on your mission and share fun facts along the way!

Table of Contents

Meet Michael Jordan	4
Learning the Game	6
A Basketball Superstar	10
Hall of Fame	20
Glossary	22
To Learn More	23
Beyond the Mission	24
Index	24

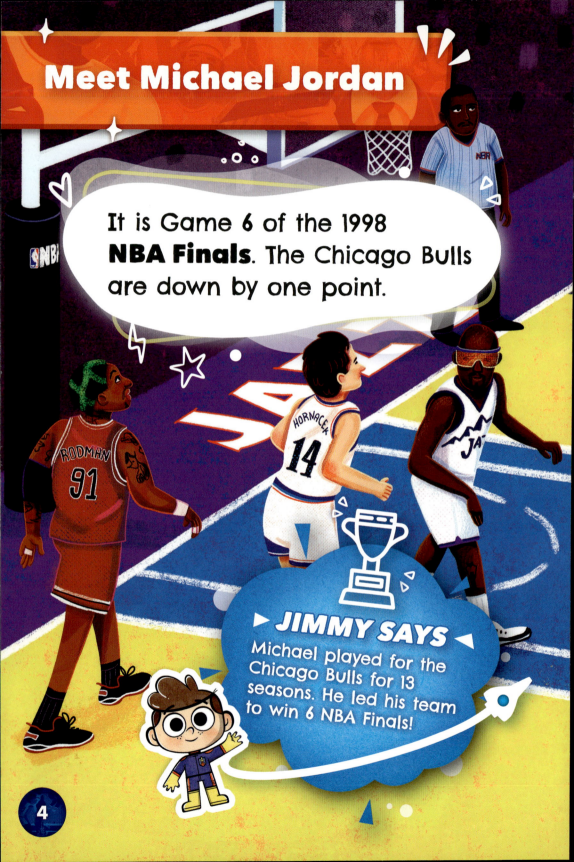

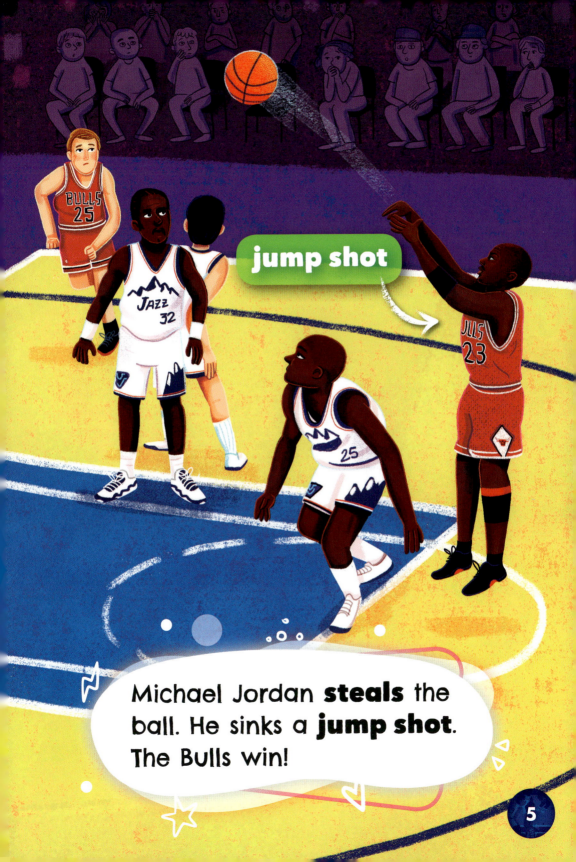

Learning the Game

Michael is in high school. He wants to play basketball. But he does not make the **varsity** team.

Michael keeps practicing. The next year, he makes the team!

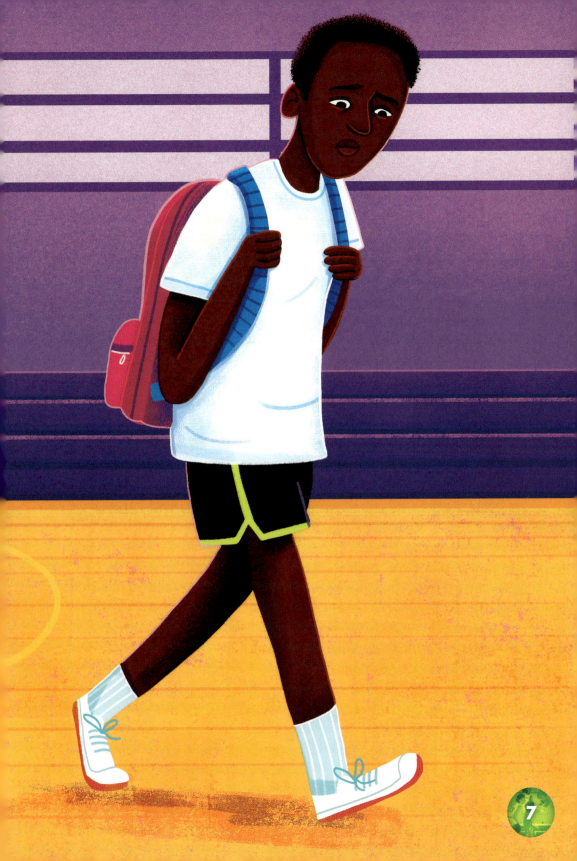

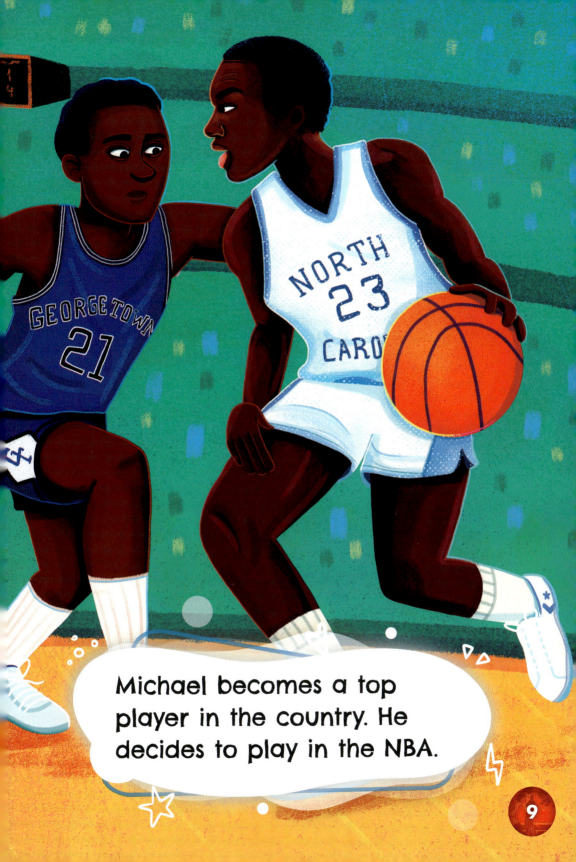

Michael becomes a top player in the country. He decides to play in the NBA.

A Basketball Superstar

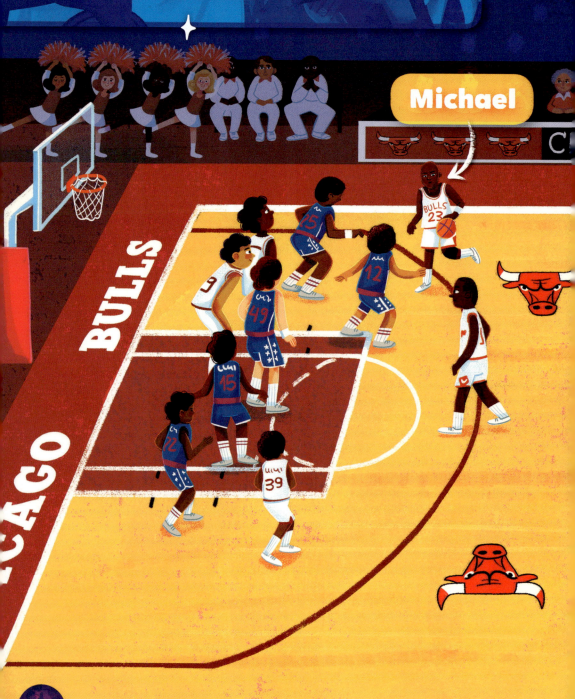

It is 1984. Michael plays for the Bulls. He ends the season as the NBA's leading scorer!

People love watching Michael play. He helps NBA ticket sales go up.

Michael is famous for leaping through the air to make plays. People call him Air Jordan!

The company Nike makes shoes called Air Jordans. The shoes are popular around the world!

JIMMY SAYS

Michael got his deal with Nike in 1984. Air Jordans made more than $100 million in their first year!

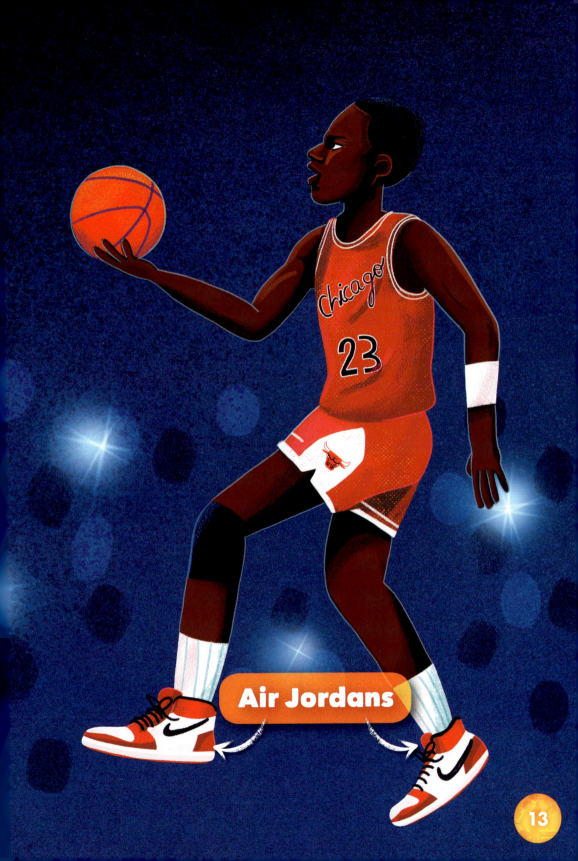

It is 1992. Michael just competed in his second **Olympic Games**. The "Dream Team" won gold!

Michael's father has died. Michael decides to leave basketball. He wants to play baseball to honor his dad.

But he misses basketball. Soon he joins the Bulls again!

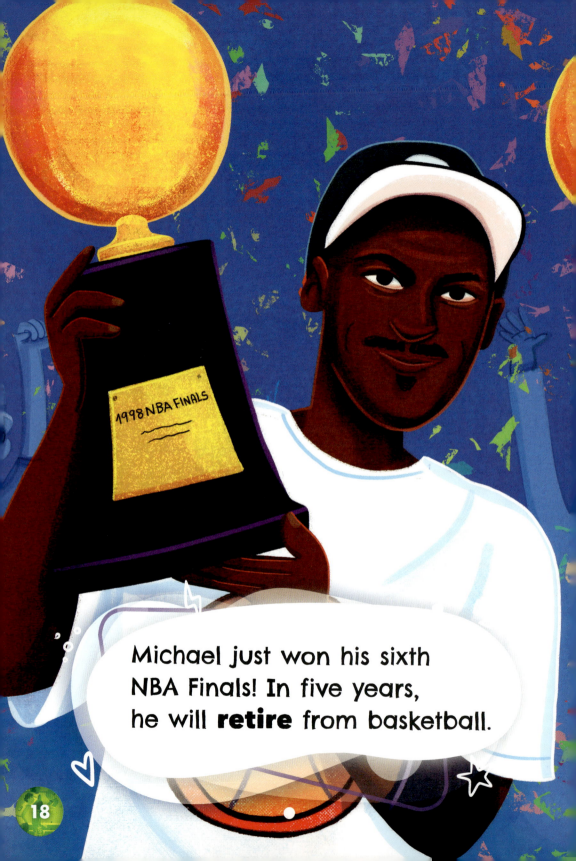

Michael just won his sixth NBA Finals! In five years, he will **retire** from basketball.

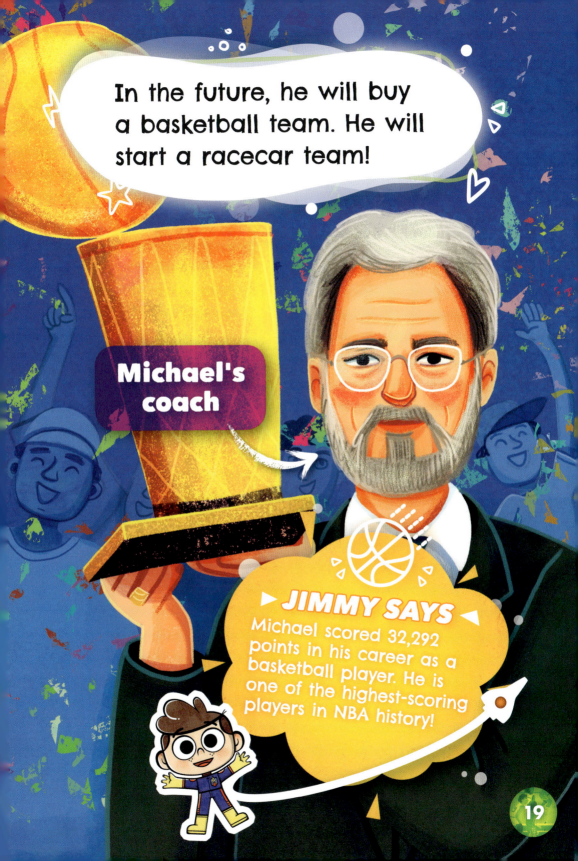

Michael Jordan Profile

Born
February 17, 1963, in Brooklyn, New York

Accomplishments
Former professional basketball player who led his team to six NBA Finals and is considered one of the best players of all time

Timeline

1984: Michael joins the Chicago Bulls

1993: Michael wins his third NBA Finals in a row

1995: Michael returns to basketball after trying out baseball

1998: Michael wins his sixth NBA Finals and is named most valuable player for the fifth time

2009: Michael is added to the Basketball Hall of Fame

Glossary

championship–a contest to decide the best team or person

college–a school that some people go to after high school

Hall of Fame–a place honoring the records of the top people in a sport

inspires–gives someone an idea about what to do or create

jump shot–a shot in which a basketball player jumps straight into the air and shoots the ball

NBA Finals–the championship series of the National Basketball Association, the professional basketball league in the United States; the National Basketball Association is often called the NBA.

Olympic Games–worldwide summer or winter sports contests held in a different country every four years

retire–to leave a job or career for good

scholarship–money given to help people attend school

steals–takes control of the ball from the opposing team

varsity–related to the top team that plays a sport in a high school or college

To Learn More

AT THE LIBRARY

Leaf, Christina. *Basketball*. Minneapolis, Minn.: Bellwether Media, 2024.

Wagner, Zelda. *Basketball Superstars*. Minneapolis, Minn.: Lerner Publications, 2025.

Whitcomb, Aidan. *Why We Love Basketball*. Mankato, Minn.: Black Rabbit Books, 2026.

ON THE WEB

FACTSURFER

Factsurfer.com gives you a safe, fun way to find more information.

1. Go to www.factsurfer.com.

2. Enter "Michael Jordan" into the search box and click 🔍.

3. Select your book cover to see a list of related content.

BEYOND THE MISSION

> WHAT FACT FROM THE BOOK DO YOU THINK WAS THE MOST INTERESTING?

> THINK ABOUT A PERSON WHO INSPIRES YOU. WHAT DO THEY INSPIRE YOU TO ACHIEVE?

> HOW DO YOU HOPE TO INSPIRE OTHER PEOPLE?

Index

Air Jordans, 12, 13
baseball, 17
basketball, 6, 8, 17, 18, 19, 20
Basketball Hall of Fame, 20
championship, 8
Chicago Bulls, 4, 5, 11, 15, 17
college, 8
"Dream Team," 14
father, 17
high school, 6
jump shot, 5
NBA, 9, 11, 19
NBA Finals, 4, 15, 18
nickname, 12
Nike, 12
Olympic Games, 14
profile, 21
racecar team, 19
retire, 18
sales, 11, 12
scholarship, 8
varsity team, 6